# Soldier From Birth

## Dr. April A. Jones

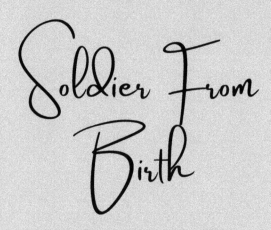

## Soldier From Birth

2021 by SAC Publishing
All rights reserved. Published in the United States by Dr. April A.
Jones, a division of Sankofa Achievement Center Inc.
Nashville, Tennessee.

www.thesac.org
Library of Congress Cataloging-Publication Data
Names: Dr. April A. Jones, Author.
Title: Soldier From Birth
Identifiers ISBN-9781737993049 (ebook), ISBN-9781737993032
(print paperback)

Jacket Illustration: Carl Burrell
Editor: Cynthia G. Jones
Guest Editor: Janie Taylor

Manufactured in the United States of America

# Foreword

*In The Name of Allah, The Beneficent, The Merciful.*

Allah (God) created the human being to struggle. And most of us don't like struggle. We like ease. But the Holy Qur'an says, after difficulty comes ease or with difficulty comes ease. You're not going to get ease without difficulty. When the difficulties come in your life, know that ease is coming. You can't run from the difficulty with a bottle in your hand, or with a reefer in your hand, or with the pipe in your hand, or with a woman by the hand thinking that this is going to console you and comfort you in your hour of difficulty. That's running; that's trying to escape.

*~Minister Farrakhan*

**SOLDIER FROM BIRTH**

# Preface

For many years I have had situations in my life that knocked me down, scared me, embarrassed me and I ran. I escaped the realities of the situation and moved on to the next option or endeavor. In truth I am still running, but as I mature, I am coming to see the purpose for my life and what God has ordained for me to do. My job is to be a humble servant and I wouldn't have believed my purpose would be to serve; obediently. It took for me to go through many difficult situations to find my ease. Now, I continue to "kick ass and take names," as I walk through my life. Just in case you don't know what that phrase means I present to you the urban dictionary meaning. "Kicking ass and taking names, a phrase used in reference to someone or something that is having multiple successes in succession. Kicking ass breaks down further as defined of kicking someone or something's ass, beating, defeating an opponent at as task. Taking names is recording a list of future contestants who will have also be beaten or defeated in a defined task.

# Preface

It also means holding people accountable for their actions in an organization. Most likely originating in the armed services, problem during Vietnam. "Kick ass" is generically applied to beating the opponent, whereas "taking names" refers to killing the enemy, or "taking their names." Indeed an action worthy of highest honor, kicking ass and taking names is the act of being unequivocally awesome. It generally involves showing people what's up, making people feeling like morons for being wrong, and defeating terrorists. It refers to an older saying, "kick ass first, take names later," or "shoot first, ask questions later." This is in general frowned upon enacting such awesomeness without "asking questions" first, however when used in this context, that much is forgiven. In Soldier From Birth, I briefly give you some background into my personal experiences. These experiences however tragic it appeared in those moments, helped me grow and mature. They helped me found the authentic guts I needed to persevere through the many tribulations that have came and still to come.

# Dedication

This book is dedicated to all the single
mothers who continuously make a way out
of no way for our children. This includes
my mother who struggled her entire life,
may she rest in peace. It doesn't matter what
the struggle is, even in the thick of it you can
persevere. With each stumbling block, the
comeback should be greater.

## Introduction

I don't have the most perfect smile. It's crooked, unaligned and beautifully flawed. When I woke up in the hospital in Memphis, I could only see out of one eye. The head nurse on duty told me to call my mother before she blew their hospital up. My mother had been calling the hospital trying to get information about my well-being after being notified of me going down on my motorcycle early that morning in Memphis, Tennessee. The hospital is not allowed to give out any information, but she was able to get some information from staff members by using her nursing jargon, lol. My mother being a L.P.N (Licensed Practiced Nurse) for over 25 years knew the drill on HIPPA rules and regulations. When I became conscious in the emergency room, staring at my leather chaps and my empty gun holster still attached to the pants, I knew the next move was to make the phone call to Deborah Jones.

With my lip busted open, orbital socket broken, stitches in my forehead, eyebrow and chin, I thought my face was ruined forever.

# Introduction

I was always told to treat all people with dignity and respect. There is no need to step on the next persons neck to reach your goal. As the saying goes, "it's enough out here for all of us to eat." Yet people rob, steal and kill for a piece of the American pie. Jealousy and envy stirs up hatred. We all know misery loves company. I learned that you have to watch the company you keep. You have to be careful who you allow in your space because people will take that inch and run a mile causing great havoc. With difficulty comes ease, but we have the wisdom, knowledge and tools within ourselves to choose and make wiser decisions. Decisions that will soften the road.

# Table of Contents

SOLDIER FROM BIRTH

Soldier Story I
Infiltrated

SOLDIER FROM BIRTH

## Soldier Story I
## Infiltrated

I was born November 18, 1981 in Chicago, Illinois. My great great great aunt Eddie had a house located at 4425 S. Ellis. We call it the low end if you are from Chicago. My mom told me her worry started when death began in the family. Her mother, my grandmother who I never had the pleasure of meeting passed away when my mom was age 12. Our neighborhood of Bronzeville on Chicago's South Side has been gentrifying for more than two decades. Gentrification, though, usually means the taking over of land from the poor or minorities by another class, usually middle to upper class whites. However, in Bronzeville where I am from, gentrification means something different. My historically black neighborhood, once the Chicago's version of Harlem, the gentrifiers were mainly black, too.

My mother recently passed, may she rest in peace, 1954-2021. My mother would say she didn't have a worry or a care in the world as she sat in the window of the family owned beauty and hair salon drinking red soda and reading magazines. This was during the time when black owned businesses bloomed and flourished in the great "Bronzeville" on 52nd and Drexel in Chicago, Illinois.

In those days you minded your business and went in your room, if company came you shut your damn mouth, you didn't get into grown people's business or you got slapped in your damn mouth, said my mother. When I was younger I think the way my mother whooped on me should've been a sin, lol. This is also during the time when we went to school in the 80's, we got spanked by the teachers as a form of discipline. This corporal punishment however controversial it may be, created a tight-knit community and a well needed village.

As I look back now as an adult, at that village, the neighborhood was a community of love and care where the neighbors looked out for one another's family. If I acted up during school, not only would I get a spanking from my teacher, but I would get a spanking from the neighbors as well as my mom once the word got out that I had to get "tightened up," at school (and the word was going to get out). People snitched then, it wasn't a death warrant. Nowadays no one wants to be a snitch, but people used to stick their noses in other people's business and for a good cause. What happened to the neighborhood watch?

There was this one day, in the fifth grade I was whole heartedly embarrassed because I stuck my nose in grown folks business and my ass caught fire! I couldn't sit down in my seat properly for the rest of the school day. My classmates thought that was the funniest shit ever, but I had learned a very valuable lesson that day as well as my classmates. The lesson was, I should abide by the same rules that my mother sets for me at home. Mind grown folks business and stay in a child's place. No other student tried Mrs. Vines like that for the rest of the school year, lol. I guess we can say, she put the fear of God in all of us with that damn ruler. It's different when you know your parents are going to side with the teacher no matter what you tell them. Nowadays, parents will run up in the school and fight the teacher before getting all the facts about disciplining their children.

Now I'm sure you want to know what exactly I did to receive this ass kicking at school that day so I will tell you. My 5th grade teacher Mrs. Vines (may she rest in peace) whom I love dearly to this day, was standing at the door speaking with another teacher, Mrs. Lott, who was my former 4th grade teacher. They were having teacher talk in the hallway. The classroom door was open and she had instructed our class to finish an assignment. Well Mrs. Lott, said something that tickled my teacher and she laughed out loud. She sounded like a hyena! Now me thinking I was the class clown stood up in class and told everybody to watch me.

As I strolled to the garbage can to throw some paper away that magically appeared because I'd just balled up a good sheet of paper out of my notebook, I loudly mocked my teachers' strange farm animal like laugh as best as I could while I passed the door to get to the trash can. I quickly bust out laughing and ran back to my seat. She immediately came in the room and asked who had done that. Well we all know the class pointed at me.

I will never forget the feeling I had when I returned to my elementary school and began teaching fourth grade next door to Mrs. Vines. We have had one of the most relevant relationships. I still quiver at the shriek sound of her husband Jim's voice when he called to tell me she had passed away. I was teaching 7th grade when I got the call from Jim. I could barely understand him as he cried to break the news to me. I felt helpless and I couldn't continue with my duties for the day.

I've considered myself a soldier from birth because according to my mother, I almost died in the hospital after I suffered from my arm infiltration. An Infiltration occurs when IV fluid or medications leak into the surrounding tissue of the skin. An infiltration can be caused by improper placement or dislodgement of a catheter.

**10**

I have always felt like there was a purpose for my life after she explained to me what happened as I aged. If you have ever seen someone with a third degree burn mark, then you have seen my arm. The skin on my right arm has been replaced with a scar that takes up half of my arm. My mother and family told the story of a crawling baby who made her way into the bathroom and ate powder laundry detergent. My older siblings were watching me while my mother was at work. She was a single mom, a hard working nurse and couldn't afford a baby sitter. She depended on the older siblings to care for the baby while she made money to pay the bills and put food on our table.

The detergent that lie next to the washing machine must have looked mighty tasty to a little hungry thing like myself. With a bloody tongue, mouth, and swollen lips, I was rushed to the hospital via ambulance. The detergent in the early 80's contained the chemical lye.

I had a reaction to the washing powder detergent, and my mother had a whirlwind of problems at the hospital. She tells the story of how when she finally arrived to the emergency room, she walked right past me laying on the stretcher because I looked almost unrecognizable in the face. The number one question that my mother was asked, yep you guessed it! Why was she not at home with me? The IV infiltrated the tissue, so much fluid infused in my arm until it cracked and burst open.

The Philippino nurse on duty was a new nurse and did not check the little infant's IV until it was too late. This occurred at the Chicago Osteopathic Hospital where I was born. The hospital no longer exist.

My mother, after retaining a lawyer and battling the hospital's legal team for over 3 years, decided to settle out of court. My chance at millions of dollars was robbed from me, lol. She settled for $50,000 out of court and our lawyer received ten thousand of that for his fees to represent us. The hospital staff failed at their duties that day because they were not watching me and if they had been properly making their rounds, they would have seen the IV swelling and improperly placed in my arm. My mother tells me I was crawling when I went into the hospital, but I was there so many months after the incident that I had learned to walk during my duration at the hospital.

I struggled with bullyism during elementary school because of this scar. "You is black and burnt as tar", classmates would cackle. "What happened to your burned up arm, were you in a fire?" I wanted to wear long sleeves all the time to cover up my arm, but one day my mother told me something that changed the way I viewed myself. She said that my arm is my arm, own it, wear it proud like a shield of honor.

**12**

My mother told me how riding the city bus home from the nursing home where she worked, she always saw these young black girls on the bus as well. She talked about the poise and good mannerism those young ladies had. She liked and enjoyed some of the conversations the young ladies were having on numerous occasions. She asked the group of young ladies what school they attended and when one of the bright young girls responded with" Trinity High School'" it was at that moment my mother made her decision. She said it didn't matter how much money and how much overtime she needed to put in on her job, she wanted to send me to this school.

For the next four years, I traveled over 3 hours back and forth to school from the Robert Taylor Homes Housing Projects in Chicago. My mother moved in with my older sister who lived there after becoming ill with pneumonia. She couldn't work for a while and to my mother's unknowing surprise, her drug addicted boyfriend at the time was stealing the saved up money she had for a rainy day to caress his drug addiction. We were evicted, fast jack. My mother's options were live on the streets or humbly ask my sister if we could come with her. My sister kept us from becoming homeless.

There were nights I recall seeing rats as big as cats on the elevators. If you have never seen a rat beat up a cat, you have not lived life, lol. Majority of the time I walked up 15 flights of stairs after coming home from school because the elevator was broken or a crack head had it held up on a floor using it for a smoking lab. I can still smell the strong stench of the piss in the dark cold hallways from people urinating in the stairwells of those project buildings.

My older brother took several bullets in his shoulder while attending high school in the Hyde Park community of Chicago. He was headed to attend his school football game as he recollects. As the car he was riding in stopped at a red light, it was exploded with loud blasts of smoking gunfire. Thanks to the Almighty he was able to live to tell the story.

Because of the violence and social inequities in our low-socioeconomic community, my mother decided to send me out of the "hood" and to the suburban area. The River-Forest community was an upper middle class to a high class socioeconomic status community. In my educational career, I began as an inner city public school student. Excelling academically despite obstacles in the streets of Chicago, I found myself taken out of the comfort and safety zone of my own people. The dynamics of teachers that looked like me had changed drastically from elementary to high school. I was now about to experience what it felt like to wear a uniform. Not just a regular uniform, but the plaid skirt and sweater uniform.

**14**

I transitioned to Trinity International Baccalaureate, an all female catholic high school. Here my leadership skills began developing, as I was captain of my varsity basketball and track team.

While attending my all girl's catholic high school in River Forest Illinois, I had to learn about all religions, not just Catholicism. I was exposed to other cultures and I met people of all diversities with rich traditions and heritage from their own families.

I learned quickly that I was not the only girl in the school who had confidence and self-pride, but now it was about utilizing that instilled foundation for excelling and competing academically at this International Baccalaureate school. I whole heartedly feel that I would not have made the ranks at that school if I wasn't already equipped and prepared for the world by first being introduced to a holistic education; a culturally relevant education and community.

Would I feel the connection that I felt now that I was about to attend my first of many white institutions of education? I was enrolled at Trinity High School which is in my terms back then, an "all-white", all girl, catholic school. My mother had a vision for my life. She found this school when I was in the 7th grade.

After graduating from high school I continued my education at Chicago State University. This was a decision made by my mother because as she explained it, all of the colleges and universities have the same books, it's all about what you put into your studies. Basically she didn't want me to go away to college. She said CSU was a prestigious college and right around the corner from our then house in the 100's. The hundreds stand for the south side of Chicago. In my opinion, the school followed a European philosophy of teaching. So, although I was attending a "Black College," I never felt the connection.

At an early age I wanted to run through obstacle courses, climb walls and low crawl under tires. Inspired by the Army commercials I saw on tv as a child. After completing my freshman year of college at Chicago State University, I decided to follow my childhood dreams. I enlisted in the United States Army after my freshman year of college. I eventually returned home from Afghanistan and continued my education at Chicago State University.

My mother was and still is a big influence on my life even more after her passing. Although her mother passed away when she was only 12 years old, her grandmother instilled that "it takes a village to raise a family" in her and she passed it on to me.

The community was a big involvement in the growth and development of her and her children. She being born in the 1950s when segregation still existed and the Black Panthers were fighting for justice. Segregation still existed and a push for education being the key to change. She forced me to keep my grades up and stay focused academically.

She encouraged me and praised my good efforts. I see students in our communities today whom lack this encouragement at home. They don't have anyone believing in them, giving them praise and driving the push for the education excellence and the scholar which is within. I always describe to my students the great feeling it is to obtain personal successes and praise their efforts. Sometimes a hug and a high-five goes a long way to someone who hasn't received it at home.

The feeling of walking across the stage and receiving my diploma was so grand and self satisfying that I wanted to do it again. I graduated and went to a private White Christian college to get my teaching license. Trinity Christian College had just what I needed to get in and out as an adult education student. I taught in the day and attended 3 hour night classes for two years. I can recall one other face that looked like mine. I was prepared for the challenge and I excelled without pause.

When I relocated to Tennessee as a single mother of two it was after my military and teaching experiences in Chicago. I moved with intention to attain a higher education, I landed back in a Black institution. Attending this school and walking around the campus of higher education once again activated my feeling a sense of pride and confidence that I had not been around for many years, since elementary school. Tennessee State University offered me the HBCU (Historically Black College and University) experience as a graduate student.

Wherever life led me and I didn't have my natural environment of African descent around, I simply pulled it from within myself and didn't need it from my academic institution. That's what it means to instill the culture within. There has been times I have heard people in my community say they don't want to do something or try something because they don't want to be the only Black person in the room. Step out of the comfort zone is my response.

# Soldier Story II
## Attempted Armed Robbery

## Soldier Story II
### Attempted Armed Robbery

At the age of 18, I was arrested for an attempted armed robbery. I made the local news headlines as I laid face planted down on the ground surrounded by tons of gun drawn police and what seemed like a circus of flashing lights.

I was preparing to enlist into the military. I had just completed my first year of college at Chicago State University and decided it was time for me to get away from Chicago. I wanted to run away from relationship and family struggles. I knew the only way I could get out of my city with no money would be with the help of Uncle Sam. Never before had I flown on an airplane, I was promised to receive a $50,000 Montgomery GI Bill which would allow me to continue my education. I also received a $5,000 cash sign-on bonus for enlisting. I was quite excited at the possibilities which awaited me in my future. Nothing was going to stop me.

My older sister relocated from the Robert Taylor Projects to Madison, Wisconsin where she hunkered down and began raising her family. I wanted to make a visit to see her and my nieces and nephews before my soon scheduled enlistment date. I called my sister and told her I was about to come spend the weekend with them.

**20**

My two and half hour trip from Chicago to Madison made me feel like I was on a fresh start of breaking free! I hit the road blasting my music in my brand new car. You couldn't tell me shit! By the time I made it to Madison my sister had alerted me that she was called in to work and the party had to pause. Well I didn't want the party to pause on her account so I decided to hang out with the next best thing who knew the town, her baby daddy. He said we could go chill at the College Club on the University of Wisconsin campus. Of course the age was 18 to get in and 21 to drink, but I had found a drivers license laying on the ground and used it to get inside the club. Hell she was black, I figured I could get away with it; and I did. The identification card belonged to a lady who was probably 20 years older than I was at the time.

Inside the club, the drinks were flowing, the vibe was right and the DJ had the building shaking. You couldn't tell me I wasn't grown. Hours had passed and it was last call for drinks. I had noticed several guys in the club, but I noticed one particular guy because he had on a loud colored shirt making him noticeable. My sister's boyfriend had been mingling throughout the night and when it was time to go he told me to go get my car out the garage and meet him on the corner.

SOLDIER FROM BIRTH

When his drunk ass got in my car he told me to follow a car down the road and block him in the cul de sac so he could talk to him. He told me to get out of the car and tell him my "brother" wanted to "holla" at him. I did what I was told to do, feeling like I was walking on the moon. I had at least 6 cups of the free Captain Morgan's Spiced Rum. I walked over to the car smiling and repeated my line. Before I knew it, my brother had walked up on us with his hand under his shirt as if it were a gun and demanded that the guy "give it up!" This guy stepped on the gas and zoomed off right into the sight of a police car which he flagged down frantically. My "brother" ran and jumped in the drivers side of my car and told me to get in! He sped off down the wrong side of the street.

The police followed my car for several blocks before flashing the lights and siren, but by that time it was at least 10 police cars trailing us. He told me to tell the police that I don't know nothing. I didn't see nothing, hear nothing! In my head I was thinking ok, got it, don't say nothing. Yep sounds like a great plan, that's the plan and I'm sticking to it. "Driver put the car in park and drop the keys out of the window. Put your hands up and step out of the car", yelled an officer through the bullhorn. My heart was pumping so hard that I just knew it would bust out of my chest and splatter everywhere.

**22**

**SOLDIER FROM BIRTH**

I couldn't keep my hands up in the air, take my seat belt off and open the door without feeling like my body would be imploded with at least 100 rounds of ammunition. Every time I heard the command, step out of the car, I tried to lower my arm to unfasten my seal belt and the command got louder and scarier, "keep your hands up!" As one of the police officers finally approached the window he noticed I had a seat belt on and told the other officers to stand down. Meanwhile "brother" was shouting in the distance "don't shoot, she doesn't have a gun!"

Once on the ground with tons of gun drawn police and what seemed like a circus of flashing lights surrounding my head as I lay face down on the concrete, all I could think about was the First 48 on tv, lol. I sat in jail for two days, my new car was impounded, and upon my release I drove my ass back to Chicago, no music playing this time feeling defeated. Wondering what's next? How can I fix this mess? Can I keep this in the closet without the military finding out is what I was really thinking.

SOLDIER FROM BIRTH

Of course I was innocent of attempted armed robbery, but the years that it took me to fight that case and being caught up in the criminal justice system to prove my innocence was soul deflating. After I plead guilty to the lessor charge of disorderly conduct, I started to forgo the process of expunging my record so these charges would not be permanently placed on my criminal record.

It has been and still is a conundrum of an issue that goes wherever I go despite the years of hard work. The number of times I have heard the question in a job interview, "why would we want to hire someone with this on their background?" Several years later I requested to see the same judge who found me guilty of disorderly conduct. I explained to him that I was trying to move forward with my life. I had children, I was a military veteran with goals and aspirations. I needed him to give me the opportunity at a fair chance in life. He granted the request.

I persevered and as I grew older and continued to experience trials and tribulations, triumphs and defeats, I found the courage to keep going. We need authentic (real) guts to defend ourselves in the world that we dwell in today. We are fighting each other, COVID-19, other countries (Taliban), police brutality and the war on drugs. Do you have what it takes to teach the next generation? As my drill sergeant use to say at Fort Jackson, South Carolina "My heart don't pump no kool-aid private!"

**24**

Soldier Story III
Skeleton Bones

SOLDIER FROM BIRTH

## Soldier Story III
### Skeleton Bones

My enlistment date was pushed back due to my criminal case, but I eventually sung like a hummingbird. Yes he did it! He told me to do this and then he told me do that and he told me to tell y'all I didn't know what the hell y'all was talking about, lol! Eventually I pleaded to a lessor charge of disorderly conduct. I finally was able to leave and start my life in the military at the age of 19. I enlisted into the U.S. Army as a Signal Support Specialist. After receiving orders to go to Korea, I learned I was pregnant and Korea was out of the question. I was ultimately stationed at Fort Campbell, Kentucky. I never explained to my sergeants about the incident. I kept my skeleton bones in my closet.

Everything that goes on in the dark will come to the light eventually. I pleaded guilty to the disorderly conduct and hot tailed it to the military and didn't look back. Meanwhile, I am 7 months pregnant with my first child speeding down the highway trying to get back to Ft. Campbell, Kentucky. I snook away from the military base for the weekend to rendezvous with my soon to be baby daddy. We are supposed to get permission to leave for the weekend, but I assumed I could run to Chicago and make it back before Monday morning formation. Well Sunday arrived and I was still in Chicago. I hot tailed it down the interstate, belly full of baby speeding.

**26**

My first thought when the state trooper hit his lights were damn I'm about to get a speeding ticket. The thoughts changed as I sat there waiting longer than I thought it usually takes for a speeding ticket. I watched as the trooper opened his drivers side door and removed his gun from its holster. What the fuck, I thought.

"Ma'am step out of the vehicle! Walk slowly backward towards my voice", he exclaimed. He notified me after placing the handcuffs on me that I had an outstanding warrant in the state of Wisconsin. He was an understanding officer, I guess considering he allowed me to sit in the front seat with my hands cuffed in the front so they could sit on my pregnant belly. Upon arrival at the Champaign Urbana jail house, I was notified that I had two counts of felony bail jumping from the attempted armed robbery case and would have to wait up to 30 days for extradition to back to Wisconsin.

They gave me sterling silver bracelets that attached from my hands down to my ankles. The suited in an orange designer jumper suit, and finished it off with some Gucci flip flops to stroll the perimeters of my cell. My cell mate offered me the floor or the top bunk, although I was pregnant, she refused to climb up to the top bunk. I laid on the floor and said fuck it.

**27**

**SOLDIER FROM BIRTH**

I was distraught thinking I would have to deliver my daughter in a jail cell. I alerted the officers that I was an active duty army soldier and would be considered AWOL (Absent Without Leave) if I didn't get in contact with my superior sergeants. Within an hour I received a phone call from my commander at the base asking me was I alright first and foremost. I was eventually released several hours later.

I was in major trouble with the military. They gave me two weeks of leave so I could return to Wisconsin and take care of my business. I didn't know I was missing court dates while I was serving on active duty. Lesson learned, what goes on in the dark will come to the light eventually. Another lesson I learned you can't run from your past. Handle my business and ensure its completely finished. I ended up losing my security clearance to work in the secure area and had to be reclassified from a signal support specialist. I basically lost my job. I went from a cozy office position troubleshooting computers and working on the battalion networks to staying outside working in the motor pool.

Soldier Story IV
Afghanistan

SOLDIER FROM BIRTH

My first field assignment came soon after September 9/11. I remember that moment while I was sitting on the couch trying to tie my shoe over my 8 month old pregnant belly. I was stationed at Fort Campbell, Kentucky and I was on the way to a routine doctors appointment at the Blanch-Field Army Hospital. While glancing at the news on my television, I saw one of Twin Towers in New York on fire and a plane had literally just crashed into the second tower, it really looked like a movie.

Oh, how quickly the military base was put on lock down and of course my appointment was cancelled. My military career was just beginning as I delivered my healthy daughter at 4 pounds 14 ounces the following month on October 28, 2001. With baby milk still swelling my breast from the decision to breast feed as much as I could before the inevitable decision came down from the President.

The decision was that we were going to war to fight against terrorism. January 2002, the executive orders came down for the 3-101st aviation battalion which I was assigned, to be deployed to Afghanistan effective immediately. I called my mother in Chicago and told her I needed her to come pick up my newborn asap. She was there the next day and I waved goodbye to them both.

While serving in Afghanistan, I was in charge of ensuring all communications remained active and stayed in commission. My responsibilities included running phone lines, setting up satellite antennas, and installing helicopter radios. I was honorably discharged in January 2003 after completing my tour of duty.

You want to know something that is just damn right awful and quite painful? Having to wear a bulletproof tactical vest, in the middle of the scorching hot desert with milk gorging breast weeping. That shit was awful. I often wondered though, if the painful moments of milk gorging meant my infant daughter was crying and hungry back home in the States? Now, 20 years later the war has ended. All American heroes are home, some gave the ultimate sacrifice. We lost. Was it worth it is my question?

SOLDIER FROM BIRTH

As I stood in the foxhole with a battle buddy on 24 hour duty guard detail, I peered at the horizon of lights moving from the Afghanis moving vehicles. I peered through my night vision goggles with my hand on the ready of the .50 Cal heavy machine gun on patrol. It was a cold night in the desert. I knew I had to stay awake so we wouldn't be ambushed and caught off guard from the Taliban.

Not only would I be jeopardizing my life, but the life of my hundreds of other battle buddies who lay rest in their tents depending on me to do my part. Secure the perimeter! I was a scared, cold, 19 year old who thought running from Chicago to the military was the best plan of action. I'm not sure which was worse in my life, the pissy project hallways and constant gang shootings or burning my own shit and using a babywipe to clean off my private parts some days.

We didn't have bathrooms in the desert, and by my unit being one of the first on ground, we were charged with setting up tents, filling sand bags, clearing the land for landmines and preparing for the next batch of troops to come replace our unit in 8 months. I was so happy when we got our orders to pack up the birds (the helicopters) and prepare for transition back to the U.S.

I returned home after being honorably discharged from my military assignment. It was time for me to raise my daughter and start my life, again. After attending Chicago State University receiving a Bachelor of Science, I remembered a suggestion made to me in a letter from my 5th grade teacher Mrs. Lestine Vines. The letter was addressed to Private First Class Jones, who was stationed in Kandahar, Afghanistan. Mrs. Vines suggested I consider a career in teaching upon a safe return from war. I took her advice because of the close connection I felt with her even as a young adult. I then switched my major to education to become a teacher.

Truth is, I wanted to become a medical doctor. Even more truth, I applied to become a Chicago police officer, but trying to fit in with the crowd, I failed the hair portion of the drug test when traces of marijuana was found present. While continuing my education upon my return from honorably serving in the U.S. Army, I went back to college. I met Abdullah Hakeem who was studying biology. Both pursuing medical careers, we married and had a son. This would be my second child. I took Shahadah (Islamic oath) in front of the mosque (Masjid al-Faatir) located at 1200 E. 47th Street in Chicago. Here I became a Muslim and joined my husband in Islam.

**33**

Soon after, I became divorced, lol and a single mother of two. Continuing my education at Trinity Christian College I went on to receive my second bachelors of the arts degree with a K-9th grade Illinois teacher license. Feeling like I needed a change, I decided to relocate myself and my children to Nashville, TN and I started teaching second grade. Here is where I began coping and self healing myself.

I found a program on Craigslist that listed an ad seeking military veterans called The Mission Continues (TMC). The nonprofit organization helps returning war veterans regain a renewed sense of purpose. The Mission Continues (TMC) assisted with giving me back hope after coming home from Afghanistan. There were so many of us veterans who came back home from the military and had no training on how to transition back into becoming a civilian again.

The Mission Continues is a national nonprofit organization that empowers veterans to serve their country in new ways. Through two innovative and action-oriented programs, The Mission Continues has helped thousands of post-9/11 veterans focus their talents and energy to tackle challenges facing us at home. Through a unique model that provides reciprocal benefit for the veterans and the local community,

The Mission Continues focuses veterans' spirit of service through volunteerism, mobilizes a network of supporters, and through service, helps solve tough challenges facing veterans and communities. By empowering veterans to serve at home, The Mission Continues seeks to change the national conversation about veterans so that this generation leaves a positive legacy of service and personal success.

I completed a six month fellowship through The Mission Continues, a national non-profit organization headquartered in St. Louis, Missouri and founded by former Navy Seal and Missouri former Republican Gov. Eric Greitens. My fellowship was completed in Nashville at an organization called NICE, the Nashville International Center for Empowerment, an organization that provides various educational and employment transitional programs for refugees and immigrants. I served in the center's youth program and adult education program as the education coordinator. I taught English language instruction and focused on raising youth test scores through applied testing strategies.

I became the platoon leader for TMC in Nashville. It was a very exciting time in my life. I was invited to The White House for Christmas one year. There were thanking military veterans. There was a huge tree in every room of the White House. It was beautiful. Food lined the middle of the rooms, buffet style. There were several bartenders set up in various locations of different rooms. **35**

While I ate, drank and fellowshipped with other veterans and awaiting for the highlight of the evening, I became a wee bit tipsy, lol. Now I do remember when Barack and Michelle entered the room, I remember the speech and the grand thank you they gave us for our service to this country. What I don't remember is after leaving the steps of the White House, how I managed to get back to my hotel room, lol. It was a magical experience to say the least!

The Mission Continues team helped me transition into my role of my own nonprofit organization. They showed me the tools and strategies to make my dream a reality. With the help of my VA disability benefits, I had the opportunity of implementing my own 501c3 non-profit organization Sankofa Achievement Center, Inc., since ending that fellowship. They helped me align my mission and vision while I continued to teach in the school system.

I knew teaching inside the classroom was not what I wanted to do to help our students. I was limited inside the school building and it was a very stressful period in my life. I had a White younger teacher envious with me because our Black students connected with me and not her. She hated the bond and eventually caused an uproar and student led riot in her classroom after I left the position and resigned.

**36**

I can remember a time I made it to work, but as soon as I parked my car, my anxiety flared up and I called the substitute hotline. I needed someone else to handle my classes for the day, as I pulled out the parking lot feeling defeated and hopeless.

I would have mood swings and was diagnosed with ADD at the age of 33. I was emotionally disconnected and detached from myself. The more I went to therapy and openly discussed the events and personal tragedies that were happening in my life, the more I realized that I did need help. I was placed on the maximum dosage of Fluoxetine. Maybe some of the traumas I've been through had indeed affected my life and my ability to teach children to the best of my ability, in some ways I thought.

I often times didn't know what benefits were being offered to me upon returning home. I did however manage to get hospital and educational benefits from the Veterans Affairs. It wasn't easy maintaining my personal life, career and school goals. I often stopped and withdrew from school during bouts of deep depression. The beauty of it all is that I still kept getting back up and persevering.

**37**

I was asked by a good friend of mine 'L', what drives me along in my journey to greatness? I began laughing because I didn't know I was on a journey to greatness as she put it. I felt put on the spot immediately, but the notion that I just really didn't know the answer made me a little nervous. I responded by saying that "I am driven because of my children." I thought that answer would suffice, but 'L refused to take a shallow response from me. She said it had nothing to do with my children, its about me being myself and defining who I am! She said your drive is the fact that you are determined to be the best you that you can be. You don't settle and you continuously are being true to yourself.

My smile suddenly turned straight and sound. Her words were powerful and effective as I was embraced and reminded that I am awesome and that one day I will see it in myself. I said I would try to smell the roses and again I was snapped at because in her words, "everybody is smelling the roses, smell the tulips, be you, be authentic, be a rock star in your own way."

During the previous conversation with my good friend, I was a second grade teacher. My son and I rode to school every morning. He was seven years old, in the second grade and he attended the same elementary school I worked at.

**38**

My daughter was 11 years old, she had just began her menstrual cycle, I was nervous and she was in the fifth grade in a school close to where I rented an apartment. I am painting the picture for you during this time of my life. Teaching second graders, raising my pre-teen and in graduate school in the evening. I was beyond a single mother who was experiencing teacher burnout by year three of teaching.

I was in the process of having my first home built, which I didn't close on in the end and I was working toward my Masters degree at Tennessee State University. My birthday was in five days and I was turning thirty-one years old. As I laid in bed, lesson planning and thinking about how one of my students had stolen my new pack of expo markers from my classroom that day, I realized teachers didn't make enough money for the headache I was feeling.

I would wake up and have severe panic attacks. Sleepless nights and depression faded in and out of my life. Being arrested for domestic violence had become a part of my criminal background. My mother always told me: "If someone hits you, kick their asses and ask questions later!" Well these days, when we hit back, we get locked up. I consistently over crowded my life's plate in order to mask up dealing with things that pained me internally.

**39**

There were times I would pull over on my way to work and have panic attacks. I would ask myself staring in the rearview mirror of the car with tears in my eyes, how do I compose myself enough to still look at one hundred 9th graders and teach effectively when I feel like a big ball of shit on the inside?

It comes a time when we are at a crossroad. We have a choice to make, road 1 or road 2? The road choices are either letting emotions, addictions or habits dictate and control our lives, or will we choose the path to get holistically healthy? I recollect when I was in the best shape of my life mentally, emotionally, spiritually and physically. When did I feel at my best and how can I get back there? It was in Army basic training at Fort Jackson, South Carolina. The devotion and motivation I exerted to complete 9 weeks of intense training helped me not only physically, but spiritually, mentally and emotionally.

# Soldier Story V
## The Domestic Fight

**SOLDIER FROM BIRTH**

*Soldier Story V*
*The Domestic Fight*

I finally had my headquarters on Jefferson street in Nashville, TN. Fisk University sat to the right of the building, Meharry Medical College was in the back yard and Tennessee State University was to the left of the building. Vanderbilt University wasn't very far either. I was so excited about grand opening day! Home Depot donated $10,000 worth of supplies to assist with the remodeling of the property. The volunteers were pouring in.

I had officially been accepted in the community as a nonprofit organization designed to help our students. I had the school system put my organization as a pickup and drop-off spot for before and after school. My community kitchen was going well, we were feeding the homeless twice a month, and providing healthy meals through the Meals At Risk program of the state. I mean I couldn't believe my dream of having my own achievement center was coming true. I met with the local politicians, and other nonprofit directors to see how better we can collectively help our students in our community.

42

I was blessed to have found a building where I could work and live. The headquarters had three bedrooms on the second floor. I could get dressed and then go downstairs and start my day. It was the perfect setup for me.

I had a partner who lived with me and assisted me with my business. The relationship was dangerous from the start. Arrested twice for domestic violence, the commissioner at the courthouse asked me why was I back in her jail after being locked up for a domestic just two months prior with the same person? You can not have a successful business like this says my bondswoman who had came and got me out the first time.

I called her office number collect and she immediately asked me "Dr. Jones, why are you back in jail'" and she called me Dr. Jones because she knew I was aspiring to become one at the time. She was speaking what I told her I wanted for my life into existence over me. She would bring her children to my after school program during the week as well, so she knew the positive things I was doing in my community.

I will never forget the day I was charged with strangulation, theft of property, and interruption of a 911 call. My mother always told me if someone puts their hands on you, to beat they ass! Well, these incidents were just that, self defense. My bond was high and the suggestion was made by my bondswoman that I sit in jail a week in order to have my bond reduced. I sat in jail for a week. It took me a year to fight my case and prove my innocence, but I got it done. Case dismissed and expunged from my record!

Standing in an empty house, destroyed. Clothes ripped up, pictures shredded, motorcycle gone from the backyard and all of my support had declined to move forward with my organization. I lost my contract with the school system and could no longer provide services and receive assistance from the school system.

The Mission Continues removed me from the Nashville Platoon Leader position. I was near homelessness after several weeks of unpaid bills. The veterans administration came to my rescue as I cried on the phone with a counselor. She came out to my SAC headquarters and we discussed in great detail how she could assist my children and I. I was given a Section-8 HUD assistance voucher so we could relocate and try to pick up the pieces. Remember with difficulty comes ease. **44**

# Soldier Story VI
## The Family Plot Thickens

SOLDIER FROM BIRTH

## Soldier Story VI
## The Family Plot Thickens

My mother became ill and could no longer work as a nurse. She needed assistance with her daily personal care. She decided to relocate from Chicago to Nashville with her brother Ed and his girlfriend Lynn. Both drug users, Ed and Lynn took my mother in on the belief that they would attain funds from her. When these two scoundrels realized that my mother was not going to allow them to manipulate and use her for financial gain they began verbally and emotionally abusing her.

I would go over daily to assist her and one day Ed wouldn't open the door for me to get in. I banged and banged on the door. My mother told me that she had not eaten, she had no water, and she was shut in her bedroom without any help with personal care. While I'm on the phone with her, she tells me that he could have passed out in his room and decided to call EMS to assist. The fire department and police came in a flash and knocked the door open.

**46**

Ed was very upset that his door was busted in by the emergency team. He alleged that I should pay for the damages to the door. He refused to answer the door for me after that incident to let me care for my mother. Ed eventually placed a restraining order against me under the demise that he and Lynn were scared for their lives because I carry a gun on my hip. They also alleged in the complaint that I had no business to come around the property, even though I was officially my mother's caregiver. On the phone my mother told me she had became sick through the night and really needed to be cleaned up.

Upon knocking on the door the next day to provide my mother daily care, Ed had the screen door locked and the main door open so he could see when I arrived at the home. When I knocked on the screen door he immediately slammed the main door shut and called the police on me. The police pulled up on me in a flash. I would have been cited and warned to remain from the property, but I again had a warrant and was arrested. This time the warrant was for an unpaid ticket and court date I missed. Once bonded out, I had to figure a way I could take care of my mother. During this time, I was now working on my dissertation and preparing to graduate. I spent nights upon nights researching, writing and editing.

One morning at about 4 am, my mother told me she really needed some help. I decided to sneaking in my mother's bedroom before the sun came up. I circled the block like a ninja on a stakeout. I parked down the street and walked to my mother's bedroom window. I then climbed up on the air conditioning unit and proceeded to lift my mother's window up. I did not know that she would not be able to see my face because of the lighting in her bedroom and the darkness from outside.

When my mother realized someone was raising her bedroom window, she started screaming bloody murder! I knew Ed and Lynn were in the next room sleep, so I tried to quickly alert my mom that it was me who was the intruder. As she still screamed, I finally got my head inside the room and told her to be quiet! knock-knock, whats wrong with you, Lynn asked excitedly. My mother quickly responded, "nothing had a bad nightmare." I went ahead and quietly cleaned my mother up using only the gallon of water she had available in the room to cleanse her. As I threw the trash bag out of the window and then climbed out whispering see you later to my mother as she thanked me for cleaning her up, I wondered when I got to work the next day, if other teachers had such adventurous lives as I.

I eventually got my mother out of that situation and gave her my bedroom in my apartment. I slept on the couch and took care of my mother until she passed away peacefully in my living room. It was very hard to watch the fire department have to remove my mother's body out of my apartment and into the funeral home van. She laid there getting cold and I laid on her chest thinking about my childhood and our relationships.

My mother didn't get a chance to see me complete my education of becoming a doctor in the field. It is because of her that I am able to take my experiences and use them in connecting and educating. We are not perfect humans, but we can learn how to take our experiences and bag them up as useable resources when necessary, especially in the field of education.

Thank you mom for instilling such deep academic ethics in me when you didn't even have a roadmap. I consider myself a soldier from birth and the mission continues. Take the highs with the lows and keep kicking ass towards your goals. You can do it! Don't give up on your goals and aspirations. In life the boxing jabs and the uppercuts will come, but learn how to bob and weave. Soldier up!

# Afterword

SOLDIER FROM BIRTH

[The following text is excerpted from a speech delivered by Minister Farrakhan at Mosque No. 12 on Oct. 20, 2002 in Philadelphia, Pa.]

*In The Name of Allah, The Beneficent, The Merciful.*

We are in a very, very serious hour. The sun is setting on this world, and as we approach the darkness of the hour, we have to be much more prayerful and much more mindful of what we think, what we say, and what we do. This is the greatest nation in the history of the present world, and our presence in this nation was fulfillment of Divine Prophecy.

As it is written in the scriptures of the Bible, "I did not try you with silver and gold. But I tried you in the furnace of affliction." We have been thoroughly tried in the 450 years of our sojourn in America and in all of our trials, in all of our pain, in all of our setbacks as a people, we have never turned on Allah (God). Even though some of us have wondered why are we suffering as we are suffering, what is it Allah (God), what have we done?

There is a scripture in the Book of John where there was a man born blind and Jesus and His disciples saw the man that was born blind and the disciples asked him, "Who did sin that this man is born blind? Did his mother sin? Did his father sin?" And Jesus said, "Neither his mother nor his father. But he is born blind that the works of God might be made manifest in him."

**50**

**SOLDIER FROM BIRTH**

Who did sin that we, as Black people, are in the condition that we are in—having eyes but not being able to see; having ears but having not really heard the word of God that would change the reality of our lives; having tongues but not being able to speak? Who did sin that the oppression on us has been harder than on any people in the annals of history?
There is something about the way Allah (God) handles what He loves.

The scripture says that those whom the Lord loveth He chastens much. What is it that Allah (God) wanted from us that He would put us in the hands of somebody that hated us as the racist, White supremacists of this nation have hated and still hate us? How, God, could you tell me that you love me and then allow my fathers to be brought out of Africa and come into something like this? Allah (God) would say, "Yes, I know it was rough on you, son; it was rough on you, daughter. But I created the human being to struggle and to face difficulties.

It is only when you struggle, it is only when you face the difficulties of your life that it brings out of you what I, the Creator, put in you. I never meant for you to have an easy time, because you can't come into Me or come unto Me except you come through trial and tribulation. You can't come into Me to be one with Me, and I with you, except that you be a purified thing. And the means of purification is not easy.

**51**

SOLDIER FROM BIRTH

The Bible talks about gold and silver and their process of purification. When you are a purifying agent, you have to put that which is being purified into the fire and you've got to hold it there. You can't hold it too long and you can't hold it too short. You've got to watch it just right. When the dross is burnt off and it's white hot but not burnt out totally, then you can fashion it and shape it into what you want it to be. Allah (God) wants to fashion a people to rule forever.

This is what Jesus was talking about when he said if you follow him you will have eternal life. It does not mean that any human being will live forever. But, he will put you in a position where you and your people and your nation and your world will never die. We have been living in a world seeing nations rise and fall, seeing empires come up and go down. But, when Allah (God) makes a people after His own likeness, you will be like the sun: You will have permanence and you will be a light for the nations of the earth.

The Qur'an says that the Ka'bah (in Mecca) is a sign. The black stone there is a sign. And just as the Ka'bah had to be rebuilt—it's an ancient, ancient house, the oldest house of worship known—so are you, the oldest people on this planet, like a house broken down that has to be rebuilt. You are a house full of idols, from which you must be purified. Taking stones and idols out of the Ka'bah is not more important than taking us away from polytheistic beliefs. Taking idols out of the holy house in Mecca is not more important than cleansing the human being from setting up rivals or partners with Allah (God) that are His own creation.

SOLDIER FROM BIRTH

It is only when we, as a people, are purified of all those things that are less than Allah (God) that we bow down and give worship so that we are washed and cleansed. The Bible teaches that you can't put new wine in an old wineskin, lest the wine skin break and the new wine spill. That means we, as human beings, have to be renewed, purified, before that new wisdom can come in. And if that new wisdom is from Allah (God) Himself, and we take it in, then He will be in us and we will be the Glory of Allah (God).

We are not that right now. We are caricatures of what Allah (God) intended when He created the human being. We have not seen what the human being is capable of accomplishing, if we were cleansed of polytheism; if we were cleansed of the worship of things, rather than the pure worship of the one God. That is why we have been in this period of great suffering.

Sisters, you have been in a period of great suffering. You are to us like Hagar was to Abraham– You are running in the wilderness, looking for help because your man is not a help for you. That's a negative condition. But, when we go to Mecca, we know Sarah was Abraham's wife and we honor and respect Sarah, but we don't follow the path of Sarah. When we go to Mecca and run between those hills, we are following the path of Hagar. Why Hagar?

Every woman wants a man that will be as Allah (God) intended a man to be. And what did Allah (God) intend a man to be in relationship to the woman? He said in the Qur'an that men are the maintainers of the woman. That's a big job. That does not mean just giving her food, clothing or shelter.

**53**

It means maintaining her in all aspects of her being, from the crown of her head to the soles of her feet. You can't maintain a woman with physical strength. You can maintain a woman with spiritual strength and with wisdom. She is not created by Allah (God) to follow you with just physical strength. She can be attracted to you that way, but she will never stay with you. She will always be looking somewhere else because her mind is not being fed as it would be by a man who is a man of God. She is created from Allah (God), and the only man that she can be loyal to, and faithful to, and honorable with is a man who is truly a man of Allah (God).Allah (God) created the human being to struggle. And most of us don't like struggle. We like ease.

But the Holy Qur'an says, after difficulty comes ease or with difficulty comes ease. You're not going to get ease without difficulty. When the difficulties come in your life, know that ease is coming. You can't run from the difficulty with a bottle in your hand, or with a reefer in your hand, or with the pipe in your hand, or with a woman by the hand thinking that this is going to console you and comfort you in your hour of difficulty. That's running; that's trying to escape. When you're in difficulty, you must say, "Yes, Allah, I'm going to face it. Whatever it is, I know You are my Patron, you are my Friend, and You will see me through this. But I've got to face it. I can't run from it." When we face the difficulty with the help of Allah (God), we find ourselves overcoming it. And every time you overcome it with the help of Allah (God), you've wiped out another idol. You won't worship this or that idol any more.

**54**

But, you know something? The Qur'an says, "I delivered you from every distress and lo you set up other God's beside Me. Surely man is ungrateful." And do you know that the first line of gratitude to show your love for Allah (God) is to show your gratitude to your mother? Whether you think your mother is all that you wanted her to be or not, you are not your mother's judge. Allah (God) did not bring you into the world to be a judge of your mother. She may be wrong, but she's your mother. She may not have been able to give you all the things that you needed or wanted, but she's your mother. She bore us with fainting and pain and she died in order to give us life because the pain of birth is equal to the pain of death.

If you are not grateful for your mother, then there is nobody that you will ever be grateful to or for, and you certainly will not be pleasing in the eyes of Allah (God). You can't be grateful to Allah (God) whom you have never seen, and be ungrateful for the blessings that He sends to you through those whom you see every day.

CPSIA information can be obtained
at www.ICGtesting.com
Printed in the USA
BVHW051600091221
623626BV00014B/584